LIFE
BEGINS
AT DEATH

LESLIE D. WEATHERHEAD

replies to questions put to him by
NORMAN FRENCH

ABINGDON PRESS
Nashville and New York

LIFE BEGINS AT DEATH

Copyright © 1969 by Denholm House Press

ISBN 0-687-21805-5
Library of Congress Catalog Card Number: 73-97570

SET UP, PRINTED, AND BOUND BY THE
PARTHENON PRESS, AT NASHVILLE,
TENNESSEE, UNITED STATES OF AMERICA

CONTENTS

FOREWORD

Is there a life after death? It seems that rather less than half of the adults in Britain believe there is; a quarter say they don't know; and the remainder believe death is the end of our existence. Predictably, among those who have no association with any church, nine out of ten either don't believe in life after death or would class themselves as "don't knows." What is more surprising is that the same is true of more than a third of those who do profess a link with one denomination or another—though probably that link is, in many cases, nominal.

From this information, revealed by Gallup Poll surveys made in recent years, it is clear that a lot of people are uncertain about a belief which has been held by the Christian Church ever since the Resurrection of Jesus Christ. But even those who do believe have questions they would dearly like answered.

At our request Mr. Norman French put to Dr. Weatherhead questions which ordinary people are asking. Does our life continue after we die? If so, what is the evidence? And what do we know about the nature of the afterlife? Will it give us a chance to make good our shortcomings and failures of this present life? Is reincarnation to be rejected out-of-hand

—or might there be "something in it"? These are but a few of the questions raised.

Dr. Weatherhead's replies are frank and stimulating. We believe they will give reassurance to many and throw light on a crucial subject.

PREAMBLE

As you read the following pages do not have in your mind the picture of a disciple consulting an oracle or a master who pretended to know all the answers.

Think rather of a group of friends sitting round the fire in Mr. Norman French's London flat discussing life after death. Mrs. French and others took part in these friendly talks and often introduced ideas which we incorporated after the tape recorder on the hearth rug was switched on. It would be unfair not to recognize their help. Further, my friend of many years, the Rev. Paul Morton-George, made certain suggestions which have been gladly incorporated.

Man's supposed survival of death is a fascinating subject and rarely dealt with from the pulpit, partly because there is so little in the Bible to go on. Yet men speculate and wonder and question. We hope that many will be helped by the answers we have given.

Instead of the usual payment to the author, the Publishers have agreed that the City Temple Psychological Clinic, which I started over thirty years ago and of which Mr. French is the Secretary, shall benefit from the proceeds of this book.

BEXHILL-ON-SEA   *Leslie D. Weatherhead*
1968

Though I am dead, grieve not for me with tears,
  Think not of death with sorrowing and fears,
I am so near that every tear you shed
    Touches and tortures me, though you think me
    dead . . .
But when you laugh and sing in glad delight,
  My soul is lifted upward to the Light:
Laugh and be glad for all that Life is giving,
  And I though dead will share your joy in LIVING.
Source Unknown

1. SOME FUNDAMENTALS

Dr. Weatherhead, why do Christians believe in life after death?

Because they accept the teaching of Christ. After all, on the cross He said to a dying revolutionary, "Today thou shalt be with me in paradise" (Luke 23:43). Men who are dying don't bluff one another. He did not say, "I *hope* we shall meet again, I have faith that we may live after this life." His words, which are recorded only by Luke the doctor, have a tremendous ring of certainty about them. Not "I hope" or "I believe," but "Today thou shalt be with me in paradise." And He says to His Father, "Father, into Thy hands I commend my spirit" (Luke 23:46). Those are not the words of a man whose personality is being obliterated by death. So if Christians accept the teaching of their Master, I think they are bound to accept that there is such a thing as life after death.

The second thing is that they feel that another life is necessary to make sense of this one. To thousands of people this life seems to have no purpose or meaning. Many have never really lived, in our sense. They have been handicapped in one way or another; indeed, none of us will die feeling we have exhausted our possibilities. Therefore many people feel that unless there's another life, this one is purposeless and all but meaningless. Another life is needed to make sense of this one.

Then another point to remember is that indubitably

Christ Himself rose from the dead. If the crucifixion had been the end of Christ it would have been the end of His religion. However we explain the *manner* of the resurrection, to me it is clear beyond all possibility of doubt that the *essential* Christ survived death and proved His survival to His followers. That made them feel that there must be a life beyond and different from life in the physical body. For those reasons Christians believe in life after death.

But Christ was unique, and because He survived death this does not necessarily mean that we will all survive death, does it?

I quite agree. We can't say that because something happens to a unique person this will necessarily happen to other persons. But it does prove that there is such a thing as life which is different from, and on another plane than, life in a physical body. Also Jesus is reported as assuring the thief, "I shall meet you again." The Fourth Gospel reports Him as saying, "I go to prepare a place for you" (John 14:2). I think survival is inherent in the nature of man's own personality, so I am not arguing that because He rose from the dead, we shall rise in the same way. Clearly we do not do so. He left an empty tomb. We do not. But for the reasons given, the evidence strongly is that we do survive and that His resurrection proves that there is another plane of being on which people live.

In view of this would you say that unless one did believe in life after death, one could not rightly call oneself a Christian?

I am very hesitant to say about any credal statement, "Unless you believe this you are no Christian." I would define a Christian as a person who tries to interpret life—or who tries to face life's demands and challenges—in Christ's spirit and live according to Christ's will as far as he can discern it. I would regard the disciples as Christians even before Jesus died. Clearly the resurrection tremendously reinforced their faith in Him and gave birth to the church which has spread throughout the world. But if a man came to me and said, "I want to be a Christian, but I am not sure about the resurrection," I would not debar him from the title "Christian." I would say, "Try and live in His spirit, examine the evidence, listen to the testimony of the saints and missionaries and martyrs." And I would hope that he would come to accept survival, Christ's survival and our own, in that way. I would not like to exclude him from the very beginning from the title "Christian" because he did not possess this particular belief.

Jesus says very little about life after death. In fact the whole Bible tells us very little about it. Why is this?

It seems to me that Jesus was reticent for various reasons. One is that if life after death is so amazing and men knew details of it they might be tempted to go into it by their own act before they had usefully

11

finished life on this plane. Another is that we just haven't the capacity to understand what it is like. You can't explain what a sunset is like to a man who is born blind and remains blind. You can say, "It's gorgeous, it's scarlet, it's crimson, it's golden," but the words have no meaning. In the next life we shall probably have capacities for entering into a completely different form of life. We shall be on a different plane, with different dimensions and greater ranges of perception.

Perhaps this illustrates what I mean. When I was a young minister I had a dear friend, an Airedale dog, with which I used to go for walks. If I patted my knee and said "Walk, boy, walk," he would wag his tail, jump up, bark, and be as excited as anything, because he knew what going for a walk meant. If I had said to him, "Now boy, we will go out and sit and enjoy the sunset," he would have expressed nothing but boredom and disappointment. In the same way, I feel that if Christ had tried to explain the next world, it would have been rather like my talking to my dog about sunsets. When Jesus talks about things that are on my plane, I can understand them and enter into them, but, to quote Him, there are "yet many things to say to you, but you cannot bear them now. You can't understand them, you can't appreciate and enter into them." I feel that this may explain His reticence.

He also said things like, "In my Father's house are many mansions: if it were not so, I would have told you" (John 14:2).

Yes, that's a hint, isn't it? The word "mansions" has been much discussed by scholars. I follow Archbishop Temple in his interpertation of the word as meaning, "inns at the side of the road." You remember the film *The Inn of the Seventh Happiness*? I remember preaching at the City Temple a sermon which I called "Inns of Increasing Happiness." I think the act of dying means that you are, as it were, at the first inn at the side of the road. You rest there for a time, and you meet your dear ones. But then you "wake up in the morning," and you find that there is a road stretching on beyond you, and that there are more inns at the side of the road. Then you progress into deeper appreciation of human fellowship, but with also a deepening appreciation of divine fellowship, as you move along that road.

If I understand you correctly, you say there is no death. We live again. Why do we then have to die? Why can't we just go on living here?

First, I would not say there in no such thing as death. Death is a fact, and it was a fact of life before man appeared on the planet. The idea of death as the result of sin which seems to haunt St. Paul is, I think, erroneous. You ask why there must be such a thing as death. The physical body wears out, or it suffers from disease. It cannot, after a certain period, be the home of the spirit. It seems to me that death is essential, as birth is essential. One marks the beginning of a period in which we inhabit a physical body, and the other marks the end of our inhabiting a physical body.

13

But I believe that one's spirit existed before birth and continues after death. The physical life, including death, is only an incident. Death is not nearly so important as we suppose. It is as unimportant as a milestone.

Yes, but I think there is a difficulty here. When I asked, "Since there is no such thing as death, why do we have to die?" you then declared that there is such a thing as death. But I have heard you use phrases like "the so-called death."

Death is certainly a fact, but it is rather a milestone on the road, or perhaps better still, embarking for another country, rather than the cessation of being. That is why I may speak of so-called death—to avoid the suggestion that it is the end of everything.

At death we simply discard this body, you mean? But what then survives? What is there of us that lives?

The essential personality, which expresses itself in some other form. You can call it an "etheric" body. The theory is that all the time we are living in this body we are as it were weaving some other kind of body— the etheric body as some people call it—in which we can manifest ourselves to our loved ones after death. And Jesus appears to have done that. He appeared to His beloved disciples, one Gospel says, "in another form." But they recognized Him and He recognized them. Paul, you remember, spoke of a "spiritual body" (I Corinthians 15:42-44).

14

Yet God gave us a terrific instinct of self-preservation. We are all afraid to die. Why should this be so?

Well, I am not afraid to die. I have lived longer than you and therefore have had more out of life. I do rather dread the interim period between my present health and my death—the period when one might be ill and useless, a burden to oneself and others. But the idea of dying, taken by itself, is attractive to me. To wake up amongst old friends with a new body that doesn't hurt anywhere and is not worn out is most attractive.

But sometimes when I am driving you in my car you are extremely nervous. Now this must be because you are afraid of a car crash. This implies that you are afraid to die.

No. I am afraid of *suffering*. Actually I am not afraid when you drive, but I am very much afraid when some other friends of mine drive. If they killed me at once I shouldn't mind. But to lie in hospital for ten weeks because they did not notice the lights had gone red is enough to fill me with fear. Indeed, I think that kind of fear is a God-given thing.

No, I am not afraid of dying. I am afraid of the suffering which may lie between my present healthy state and death. I think death is a tremendous adventure—a gateway into a new life, in which you have further powers, deeper joys, and wonderful horizons.

I still want to press the question, Why then do we have to cling so ardently to this life? Why can't we just go ahead and rush into the next if it is going to be that much more lovely than here?

Because this life has something to teach us. As I see it, it is one of the lower forms in God's school, and you have to pass through this form and you have to pass the exams at the end of it to graduate into the next. If you were so eager to leave this life that you took your own life when you might have served others and learned many valuable lessons, this would be wrong. God has surely given us the instinct of self-preservation because He has something for us to do in this life *which can only be learned in this life*. So we cling to it. It's instinctive. It's an innate urge to live and to continue to live as long as you healthily can.

Are you saying that this life is a preparation for a fuller life after death?

I think that is what it is for.

During your ministry, you must have been at the death-bed of many people. Would you feel there is any justification for having this terrible fear of death at the end, having seen people die?

I think there is no such justification. I have seen a number of people die, and I have made inquiries of nurses and doctors. You'll appreciate that most people die following a state of unconsciousness. Either they are in a coma or are drugged. But I have sat at the bedside of a man who was dying and conscious to the end. He gripped my hand, and I must have gripped his more tightly than I thought I was doing, for he said, "Don't hold me back. I can see through the gates. It's marvelous."

If you had seen, as I have, a woman so ill that she couldn't lift her head from the pillow, if you had seen her sit up, her eyes open with tremendous delight, and joy in her face, if you had heard her call the name of a beloved husband who had been dead twenty years, you would find it strangely convincing. People may say it was probably a hallucination, or a trick of the brain. All I can say is that it was very convincing to the on-looker that she really was in touch with the beloved dead and that he was coming back to welcome her.

I have collected dozens of incidents which point to man's survival of death.

My own father-in-law spoke continually, when he was dying, of the presence of a daughter who had been dead for years. I remember also the case of a sister in one of our big teaching hospitals, who was looking after a dying woman, whose son committed suicide during the fatal illness of his mother, and therefore she was never told (I think his name was Michael). Yet she said to the sister, who told me about it, "Do you know, Michael has been with me all day today." Now, she did not know he had taken his life, so she was not imagining things, and I think that very likely he *was* near his mother.

17

Consider all these situations together and also remember that, at any rate in my inquiries made over
a long period of years, never once has anybody died
in mental unhappiness. They can show fear before
the end; they can dread the idea of dying, but, if they
are conscious to the last, the evidence is that it is an
extremely happy experience. A physician to the Royal
family, when he was dying said, "If I had strength
to hold a pen I would tell mankind what a wonderful thing it is to die."

*In spite of this, most people mourn when they are
separated from their loved ones by death. I think the
Christian faith teaches us that this is mere selfishness,
and therefore sinful, and that wearing black for mourning is superstitious and dates back from ancient times.
What would you say about that?*

I wouldn't call it sinful. I think it's very natural for
people who have loved someone very dearly to miss
them terribly. You miss their physical presence, their
voice, their eyes, their kiss, their radiant personality,
their unhindered friendship.

But I would say two things about it. We ought to
train ourselves to think something like this. "If this
loved one of mine had gone to Australia I should be
very sorry to miss him, but I should know that I should
meet him again and that he was living and fulfilling
a purpose and possibly doing something he had always
wanted to do. No less is true if he has gone to the
next life."

The second thing is that the evidence of those who

18

have studied psychical research indicates that over-mourning, over-grief, and exaggerated sadness can hold the so-called dead back from entering into a happiness which they would otherwise have. If we could say to ourselves, "I am terribly sorry and I feel very lonely, but I shall meet him again, and I want to rejoice in his freedom from disease and pain," I think then we should cheer ourselves up and we should probably do a service to the dead.

You have spoken of people dying in bed and having died after a long illness and often in unconsciousness; but what about the person who is knocked down in the street or killed through other calamities? Do you feel he is equally prepared to die, and dies as happily?

No. I think if a person is knocked down and killed he certainly is not prepared to die except in so far as his life and faith up to then have made him so. From the evidence of psychic research it seems that such people do not realize for some time that they *are* dead and it may take them a little time to realize that they are what is called "dead" and to adjust to another life. But that does not mean that entry into another world is unhappy or unpleasant for them. In all but the physical sense they go on where they left off.

Have you any examples to give of this?

I was thinking of examples like those Major Tudor Pole gives in one of his books (I think it is *The Silent*

Road). He tells of a company commander who was shot early in a day's battle, but who was seen and heard by his men later to be still leading them on when presumably they did not know he was dead.

The same author tells of people who themselves did not know they were dead. I remember talking with a very distinguished man who told me of a friend of his who had allegedly come to him after his (the friend's) death. He said, "I was killed by a bus in the Strand, but I did not know I was dead. I went on to my office, and while I was there my partner said, 'I wonder what has happened to Sam, he's never late. What can have happened?' So I said to him, 'I'm here; don't worry; I am standing near you,' but he took no notice. Then I realized that there was something odd about the situation. Somebody else came, as it appeared to me, right through the wall and said, 'Look, old man, you're dead; but so am I. Come along and I'll explain things to you.' Then he said that I would gradually realize that I was what they called dead. But it took me a long time to realize this."

I believe that if one dies suddenly like people who are shot or fall down a cliff or meet with an accident it probably does take some time for them to realize that they are what is known as dead. But we mustn't surround the whole idea of dying with a melancholy atmosphere. They are still living; there is no such thing as death regarded as the end. It is only moving from one room in the Father's home to another room.

Would you tell us in detail why we are here? What is the purpose of this life?

20

It's a complicated question. I think we are here as though we were children in a school who had things to learn in order to fit themselves for a further life beyond schooldays. I view the earth life as one of the lower forms in God's school, and I think here we have to face certain problems, master certain temptations, overcome certain difficulties, equip ourselves for a further life which I take to be an increasing richness of communion with God.

Does this life decide our destiny for the next?

The fact of dying, in itself, does not seem to me to determine whether you go to hell or you go to heaven, although this is the view of certain Christian sects amongst us. I believe that when you die you go on where you left off. I can't believe that the accident of dying, which may be a drunken taxi driver's mistake or a fall of coal in the pit or some other chance happening, determines our eternal destiny. Probably you would find that in the next phase spiritual values seem more important. I hope it is so. You obviously leave behind you those demands which only the body makes, but the spiritual life seems more important and you long more and more to enter into it.

That's why it seems wise to try to look over our luggage, as it were, and make sure that we are not carrying something that we shan't be able to take past the port of departure, if you see what I mean. I feel there may be an Angel on the quay who looks at us and says, "Well, you won't want this and you

21

won't want that—sex appeal, intellectual brilliance, social status, the accumulation of wealth." These things don't count for anything, surely. Not what I have done, but *what I have become through my doing* seems of immense importance. If I can develop humility and loving, and I would also add humor, and a desire to serve others, these seem to me immensely important bits of luggage to carry. Is that the sort of thing you mean?

Yes. What you are saying is that we are already spirit here and now and that the way in which we lead our lives here does decide our destiny in the next life?

Yes, but it determines our destiny only in the same way that a man at the University who takes his degree determines the abilities that he can use when he follows his profession. But that does not mean that at death you remain forever what you are and cannot make any progress.

Could you explain what Jesus meant by "eternal life"?

I don't think He meant a life that merely goes on forever and ever and ever. That is to say, the quality of eternal life is not determined by length; it is determined by depth. Jesus meant by eternal life the life which the spirit of man finds when it is in communion with God.

Some people seem to think that eternal life starts only when we die, but surely this isn't true?

No. The teaching of the gospels, especially of the Fourth Gospel, is that eternal life is to be thought of as quality and not quantity; not in endless years but in a quality of communion with God which clearly begins now. You know, people talk about the afterlife and they say, "He's gone to be with God." But he always has been with God, and the highest heaven doesn't mean that God exists in any fuller measure. It can only mean that our power of communion deepens. But one of the marvelous things about the Christian gospel is that the offer of eternal life is here and now. (John 5:24.)

For example, where the first three Gospels use the phrase "enter the Kingdom of heaven" the Fourth Gospel speaks of "having eternal life." This goes to show that eternal life is a matter of the quality of one's living and not just going on forever and ever.

Can you describe this quality of life?

I feel that the Gospel writers mean life in harmony with God. Life always is correspondence with the relevant environment. The life of my eye is the ability to correspond with its relevant environment, which is light. The life of my ear ceases if its correspondence with sound ceases. Similarly the life of the soul is its correspondence with its relevant environment— which is God.

Does this mean that where there is no communion with God eternal life is impossible? As I see it, a man

23

can be alive here and have no communion with God, and yet he will have a soul nevertheless. His soul will go on after he dies, after he lays down his physical body. But you have just now been saying that the life of the soul depends on communion with God— which this man has not had.

The answer is, I think, that there is no one who is entirely cut off from God. We are so apt to think of communing with God as something in terms only of religion. But there isn't any living soul, surely, in this world who is entirely blocked from the sense of beauty, from emotions roused by music, from love, from appreciation of various forms of art? In all these ways God is in touch with man. Communion with God isn't necessarily limited to prayer, going to church, and similar things, important though these are.

He who, for example, perceives beauty or shows compassion is in living communion with God even though it may be that he has not recognized it as such. It is inarticulate religion, but it's religion none the less.

But does such a person experience "eternal life" ?

The way to it is always open to him. But he has not yet known it anything like as fully as he could do.

How can we help him to know it better?

One way, I am sure, is to help him to see that his appreciation of beauty, love, and also of truth is in fact an experience of God.

2. IS THERE PROOF OF SURVIVAL?

Dr. Weatherhead, I am sure that there are vast numbers of people, especially young people, who find it very difficult to accept honestly in their own minds that there is a life after death, and yet human nature itself is evidence of immortality, isn't it?

Indeed it is.

Science has established surely beyond any reasonable doubt that man has evolved out of nature and that he is raised above nature by his moral and spiritual ideals. Surely therefore it is unreasonable to believe that death is the end? You say in one of your books that if death were the end it would be as if the universe had produced its supreme creation and then flung it away like a capricious child throws away its toy. Could you enlarge on that idea? I am sure it would be helpful to many people.

I think that no man at his death has exhausted his possibilities, and few men have even started to use their highest powers, such as the power to love, really to love. If there is no further plane on which those possibilities can be expressed, and if there is no opportunity to do the things of which man is capable, essentially capable by being man, then it seems to me that the whole of human life is irrational. Powers would have been created and then denied any expression.

But even if there is a universal belief that immortality is a fact, this does not necessarily make it a fact, does it?

No, it certainly doesn't. Yet in a rational universe a universal longing seems to me to be a kind of signpost pointing in the direction of the satisfaction of the wish. If the world is a rational place, the fact that I feel hungry seems to me to point to the fact that there is such a thing as food. The terrific hunger of sex seems, in a rational world, to point to the fact that there is such a thing as a mate and the happiness of sexual fulfillment. Similarly the desire to go on after death at any rate points in the direction that it is likely. If you find ten signposts all pointing in a certain direction, it is fairly logical to suppose that there is a village there. Do you know what I mean?

I do. But on the other hand our desire for sex and our desire for food are much stronger than our desire for the next world. In fact, we are most reluctant to go into the next world.

Well, you're reluctant because you're young. But I myself find that my desire to explore another world is far stronger for instance than my desire for food. And the idea that because a thing is wishful thinking, that is an argument against it, is a fallacy. If my beloved is terribly ill, I wish she would recover. That doesn't mean that she won't recover.

I think of a little boy separated from his family in the terrible war days and being—what did they

26

call them?—an "evacuee," poor little kid. He dreamed literally night after night that he had a father and a family and love. This was wishful thinking, but it did not mean that there wasn't a family and father and love. In the end, thank God, he was reunited with his family, and the reality was lovelier than the dream. In the same way so many thinkers have said that it's the passion to live again that makes us believe that we must live again, and the wishful thought is not a denial that it can be true. Wishful thinking does not mean that it is ridiculous.

No, but it doesn't prove it either.

No, it doesn't prove it. But in a rational world it makes it likely.

Then would you say there is any proof of life after death?

I feel frankly that in spiritualism (as it is usually understood) there is a lot of nonsense, quackery, tomfoolery, and deceit. But having done all the reading I have been able to do on the theme, I do firmly think that the spiritualists have proved their case. There are some situations which go to show that communion with the so-called dead is established, that any other hypothesis is less likely, less probable. I regard it now as proved that man lives after death, that his consciousness is not not just the result of chemical changes in his brain and perishes with his brain but has an individual existence which, during his earth-life, has *used* the brain.

Somebody thought he was very, very clever when he said that our consciousness is like the light of the candle, and when the candle is used up the light goes out. And this was alleged to be a proof that man's consciousness dies when the physical thing that gave it body, so to speak, perishes. Like the candle. But the very illustration is feeble, because the light of the candle is still in the universe. If you had instruments fast enough and sensitive enough you could recover that light. It's still vibrating through the universe after the candle itself is burnt out.

And I see no reason to suppose that man's consciousness, though it *uses* a brain, dies *with* that brain, any more than a man who is a violinist and expresses himself through his violin ceases to be a musician if you smash his violin. What's to stop him picking up another instrument and playing on that? When I die and this body rots in the grave and is absorbed into the matter of the universe, what is to stop my consciousness picking up some other instrument, such as an etheric body, and using that? You will find that this was Paul's idea if you read I Corinthians 15. Paul is very sound and modern in this when he says that God gives the soul another body in which it can express itself. The corn of the wheat falls into the ground and dies, but we know that life springs up again in a different way.

Yes, and if this were not so, this planet of ours would surely be so overpopulated that we could just not cope with all the beings in it?

You mean, if we lived without dying? Yes, a terrible thought.

And so the "etheric body" takes up no room?

No, no. A spirit doesn't occupy space and an etheric body doesn't. While we are thinking about this theme, an analogy that appeals to me very much is one which came home to me when I was walking on the Scottish moors with my son and we found a lark's nest. In it were eggs ready to hatch. You could even put the egg to your ear and hear the tapping of the little beak. Within that egg was a bird with all the mechanism of eyes, ears, voice. Now, if death is the end of man it seems to me as silly, as irrational, as stupid as if every egg were crushed before it hatched. Just as in that egg were latent abilities to sing, to see, to soar, so man's abilities are not extinguished when he dies. They are set free for further use. He has longings and yearnings and possibilities which can find their functioning only in a life beyond this. It makes sense of things, doesn't it?

It does to me, yes. What do spiritualists mean when they talk about "guides"? Are the guides what we Christians would call guardian angels?

You know much more about spiritualism than I do. I thought guides were thought of as spirits of people who had passed over from this side and who helped their fellow mortals to make contact with the other world. I would hesitate to identify them with the an-

29

gels. In the communion service we say, "Therefore with Angels and Archangels and all the company of heaven we laud and magnify Thy glorious name, evermore praising Thee and saying, Holy, Holy, Holy" —this seems to me a far finer and wider conception than the spiritualists have when they talk about guides, though in my own thought there is room for both. Perhaps those who have died may find a delightful and valuable bit of service in attending to the dying and in helping communication between the living and the dead, which, as we so well know, is full of pitfalls and difficulties. Consequently, I, for one, do not recommend the bereaved person, unless he be emotionally very stable, to seek comfort in a séance.

3. AFTER DEATH—WHAT IS IT LIKE?

Could you give us any indication of what life might be like on the next plane?

I have studied all the literature I could on what is loosely called Spiritualism. I am not a spiritualist, but I am a member of the Society for Psychical Research, and I feel strongly that *when* we have men with all the discipline of the modern scientist applying their methods and powers to exploring the field loosely called psychic research, we shall reap an enormous benefit, a far richer harvest than we have reaped from our modern flirtation with physics and chemistry and so on. In the literature that I have read, anything which seems an *authentic* message from "the other side" is unanimous in saying it's marvelous. I could quote case after case. Think of F. W. H. Myers saying, through a reputable medium like Geraldine Cummins, "If only I could tell you what it's like; I just haven't the words to tell you how marvelous it is; the sense of beauty, the sense of freedom, the sense of love," and so on. I do really believe that Paul was making a right guess when he quoted, "Eye has not seen nor ear heard, neither have entered into the heart of man the things that God has prepared for them that love Him" (I Corinthians 2:9).

Would you say that we develop in life after death?

Oh, definitely. If there is life there must be growth. There can't be a thing called the static soul in another life any more than in this life. Either you are going up or going down in this life and you remain "you," and because somebody or something kills your body that will not alter the fact that you are "you," and you will continue to go up or down.

Does this apply to those who do not die in faith as well as to those who do?

I confess that I am rather hesitant about this. I think it is terribly hard to assess the spiritual condition a man is in by such terms as that. The branch of the church which refers to "dying in faith" believes that at death your destiny is settled; that what you are at the point of death you are for all eternity. Some are going to be in Heaven and some are going to be in Hell. This I don't agree with at all, and I don't think it is true to the spirit and message of Jesus. A lot of people who deny the faith have never really had the faith fairly put to them. On the other hand a lot of people who profess a great deal and say they are "saved" don't impress me as having caught the spirit of Christ.

Then again, what are you going to do about all the people who haven't had any chance of understanding what Christ is talking about? What about the people of other faiths? Surely there is a way to God's Heaven for the Buddhists and the Hindus and the Mohammedans? What are you going to do about little children who die before religion has any meaning at all? I can only suggest that at death we go on spiritually where we left off.

This then applies to the child who dies in infancy and has had no opportunity for soul growth; he goes on from where he left off?

Yes, and if you say he left off before he could have made any spiritual progress, surely there are helpers waiting for him on the other side. Nor do I exclude the idea that the child may come back again in some other life and find reality there, and take the exams, so to speak, which physical life demands from us.

Would you say that we sinners get a second chance?

Not only a second chance but a thousand chances. If the soul goes on where it left off and still has free will, it has power of choice. It can make the choice of climbing higher, or it can make the choice of indifference, or it can make the choice of descending lower. You can't have a free human spirit *compelled* to climb the higher way, can you?

No. Is the parable of Dives and Lazarus relevant here (Luke 16:19-31)?

I think it's relevant if you don't push it too far. It's rather dangerous to take any parable of Jesus, when it was spoken in a certain circumstance for certain people, and apply it to all circumstances and all people.

For instance, the rich young ruler could be quoted as though the possession of wealth was unchristian and unworthy. But Jesus was really saying to one man, "This is what is in the way of your spiritual

33

progress." He cannot have meant to apply it to all such people, for Jesus Himself depended on rich people, accepted the hospitality of rich men, and praised Abraham who was one of the richest men in the Bible.

Now here is the parable of Dives and Lazarus. Dives is rich and feasting and the poor beggar Lazarus is sitting in the road outside in rags, and also in pain and suffering. There were no serviettes and table napkins in those days, and the rich man used pieces of bread to clean his fingers and then tossed them out of the window behind him. Lazarus, the poor beggar, picks them up and they become his only means of sustenance. Then, says Jesus, they both die and pass into another world and the poor beggar is comforted and Dives is tormented. But he is not tormented by some outside devil. He is tormented by the insight that he now gains of what a selfish, thoughtless person he was, and how inconsiderate he had been to others.

Now, in the parable Jesus says that the rich man pleaded with Abraham and said, "Do send somebody to tell my brothers lest 'they also come to this place of torment.'" In other words, "Do show them what I have now learned or else their consciences will torment them as mine is now tormented."

And Jesus makes Abraham say it wouldn't be any good; they would not take any notice even if one rose from the dead. The parable seems to me to say that you can't thrust insight on a person. He has to go through experiences himself, which can be very painful (equals Hell) until he himself discovers the truth about things. You asked if there is progress. Well, the rich man had already made progress because at least he is concerned about his brothers. Before, he wasn't concerned about anybody, except himself. He had no thought for his brothers, no thought for the beggar outside. The parable shows that at last, after death, he begins to think, "Oh dear, what about my poor brothers?" This is advance isn't it?

Yes, definite advance; and it is also comforting to learn that a child who died without having been given the opportunity to grow here also has the chance to advance there. Which leads me to wonder whether the mother who must love this child would meet her child again.

The answer is obviously, Yes, or it would be no heaven for the mother.

But then the child grows; the child does not remain a baby. Will the mother recognize her baby?

Yes, she certainly will.

In the same way people say, "Look, my loved one died twenty years ago; he will have made immense progress in the spiritual world. If I die tomorrow, is he going to be so far advanced that we can't really join up together again? He will be so far ahead of me." But this is, in a way, "geographical" thinking, isn't it?

I tend to see things in pictures. I imagine a brilliant

mathematician—let's imagine a professor in mathematics at Oxford, a person I knew. And let us imagine that he is sitting in his study and at the table in his study his little boy is laboriously doing his sums. Now, there is an enormous gap between them; one is a professor of mathematics, the other is a child working out a simple addition sum. And you say, how can they have fellowship? He will never catch up with his father. But their *love* relationship is not interfered with. Jesus said to the dying man of the cross, "Today you will be with me" (Luke 23:43). Well, there was an enormous gap between them in terms of spiritual advancement, but nevertheless Jesus promised that He would be with him. There is no gap in love, is there?

No. Love is probably the one essential; it bridges all gaps.

Exactly. I think it is important to reassure people of the reality of reunion, of the joy of it, of the amazing happiness of it, however they may differ in spiritual attainment. Those who love will delight in expressing their love by helping their loved ones.

This raises another problem of the person who has been happily married and one of the partners dies and the remaining partner marries again. Which of these two partners are they going to be happy with in the afterlife?

Well, yes, Jesus answered that. He said that in the resurrection there is neither marriage nor giving in marriage, but they "are as the angels" (Mark 12:25). I take that to mean that they are in quite a different relationship. A great part of the marriage union is the physical union, the physical attraction that one has for the other. Surely that fades out. I would have thought that we are in a closer, even more loving relationship, devoid of sex and physical attraction, and a love-relationship which need not be restricted to one person.

This is what is so confusing. We are so possessive here with our love and think it is for us only and no-body else must have it. I think when we get over there we will understand love more fully, and will see that we can love many people.

Yes, but I would think that a husband and wife who have been very closely allied in spirit as well as body on this side have a special relationship. I don't see myself as being in exactly the same relationship to five hundred other women I have known as I am to my wife. Unless one of us repudiates it, I should think our lives will be entwined in a relationship of special closeness and increasing richness.

But that is possessive . . .

Not necessarily. The mere fact of marriage does not in itself mean union on the other side. Surely you are close only to those you love, and if a marriage has been only a semblance, if it has only been, "Oh, let's stick together for the children's sake"; if it has only been a convenient way of avoiding what the Joneses might think about a break-up, then I think it will provide no link, no power at all on the other side. There are of course far too many marriages based on that premise.

Exactly, and there is far too little understanding of what love really is—think for example of I Corinthians 13—all of which will be given to us with greater understanding in the life after death.

Dr. Weatherhead, could you enlarge a little more about what the next life is like?

Well, it's bound to be speculation, and Jesus Himself was very reticent about it. Nor are the researches of the Society for Psychic Research very illuminating, and nobody knows of course what the "etheric body" is like, and what means of manifestation we have on the other side. I would agree with those who speculate that all the time we are alive in this life we are weaving a sort of etheric counterpart, and that death simply means that we put down the physical part of our nature and continue our life in the etheric body. Now, that's a phrase that covers ignorance, and I can't pretend to dispel that ignorance very much. It seems to me likely that at first we do not realize that we are dead. You will remember my mentioning that a lot of the Psychical Research Society's investigations and reports from "the other side" made that point. It may indeed be as some scientists have suggested that there is—I don't know how to put it—a body functioning with different rates of vibration, which may have something physical about it and something psychical or spiritual about it, and from that we pass on to what is a more purely spiritual existence, but containing immense possibilities of enjoying beauty and of helping others.

But I think we have a glimpse of the quality of that life on this side of death. For instance, there are moments of tremendous spiritual exaltation which I expect nearly everybody has had. Or think of a lonely girl who suddenly finds herself truly loved, and gives her love in return, and she feels secure and wanted, and of supreme importance to somebody who seeks to share her life. Isn't that experience of being loved and having a chance fully to express love, a foretaste of Heaven?

Yes, I should think it probably is.

Some people find it in music. I am not educated in music enough to know, but some of my friends seem lifted, as they say, to a seventh heaven, by the work of the great masters. Wouldn't you think that was so? Wordsworth had a theory—I think he got it from Plato—which attracts me very much; that every beautiful thing you see on earth is a translation into matter of some unseen reality in the other world, in the world of spirit. When you look at a flower, and admire its beauty, or when you listen to music and are thrilled by it, you are really getting a glimpse through the

39

senses of a reality far greater and tremendously beautiful in the realm of spirit. I think that's an attractive idea.

Could one say that in such experience one is getting a view of God?

Yes, I think any experience of truth or beauty or goodness or love *is* an experience of God.

Dr. Weatherhead, we are constantly impressing on the minds of young people that we are now here not only as physical bodies, but that we have a mind and we have a spirit. We know the necessity for feeding their spirits and cultivating their spiritual life in order to live a decent life and to build up character. Now, I think many of them might be confused when we also bring in terms like "soul" and "essential personality," which goes on after we have put down these physical frames of ours. Could you say something to make that clear to young people?

I will do the best I can. My own vision is so limited that it's a bit difficult. I would equate soul and spirit. I would say that man is a trinity in unity. He is body, mind, and spirit. Now the body clearly is that physical part of ourselves through which we make contact with the outside world. The mind is that unseen immaterial part of man by which he expresses thoughts. He has mind in common with the animals, although it is much more developed, and whereas the animal knows, man *knows* that he knows. He is a self-conscious personality. Now the brain is to be remembered as part of the body. I use my brain to think as I use my hands to feel, and the fact that when I die my body, including my brain, falls into dust doesn't mean that my mind stops existing, as I mentioned earlier, any more than when a violinist smashes his violin he ceases to be a musician. He could go and pick up another instrument and play that. And I believe that I survive death but instead of having a brain with which to think and communicate, I have some other kind of instrument which is suitable to my new environment.

Now the spirit (the soul and spirit I take to be the same) I regard as that part of the mind with which I can worship, that part of my immaterial being that is capable of communion with God. That's how I distinguish body, mind, and spirit. When one talks about the "essential personality," this is what I believe survives. I mean that immaterial part of myself that is the real "me."

It has *used* a body, it has *used* a brain, but it is essentially mind-spirit.

Yes, I think that has made it somewhat clearer. But there is still another complication because we bring in this term "etheric body." So am I right, then in thinking that the mind and spirit and essential personality are all one with the etheric body?

Yes, I speculate that, just as in this world we need a body with which to express ourselves, when we pass into the next sphere of being, there must be some means of manifestation, which I call the etheric body. Otherwise I would not be able to communicate with my loved ones, I would not be able to have fellowship with others, I would not be able to serve others, and there must be some means (which I call the etheric body) by which I recognize my friends in another world and am recognized by them, and differentiated from other spirits.

You see, if any existing animal knew only two dimensions—say length and breadth—then something that also had height would be unperceivable by that animal because it would be manifested in a dimension foreign to itself. May it not be that when we pass into another life there are other dimensions in which being can be manifested? So that what is impossible for us to see and register by the senses we now have, would be perceptible in a life in which there was another dimension?

To sum up, there must be some form of manifestation after we have finished with this body by which we can express ourselves, and through which we can be recognized.

Yes. Would an etheric body be a right term to use when referring to the resurrection of the body of Jesus?

I should think so. It was evidently a body manifesting itself in a very different way from our own; perceptible to some, imperceptible to others; able to pass through closed doors; able to travel great distances. I think it would be quite fair to call it an etheric body; though in a sense that phrase is only a label for our ignorance.

So to recap, on this plane we have the physical body which can suffer physical illnesses and have physical sensations; we have a mind with which we can think and we can also have mental illnesses. So we have a G.P. to treat the physical body, a psychiatrist to treat the mind, and a minister to treat the soul.

This is ideal, yes, if they all know their jobs! And ideally if they cooperate as a team.

But even in this life the different parts of our personalities are all interwoven, aren't they, and they can't be separated one from the other really, and shouldn't be separated in treatment?

Oh, I entirely agree, and this was taught by Plato years before Christ. You must deal with the *whole* man, he said, including the soul. The soul can be sick and make the body and mind sick, just as much as the body and mind can be sick from physical causes alone.

Dr. Weatherhead, there is a widespread fear that people who die mentally sick go into the next life mentally ill. This isn't true, is it?

No, I am sure it isn't. For one thing, a great deal of mental illness is due to physical causes so that when

43

you lay down the physical body, you know you have finished with that. But the kind of illustration that I like to use is to think of a mentally ill patient as a man sitting in a room with the kind of crinkly glass in the windows that you use for bathrooms and such like. Let's suppose he is locked in and can't get out. When he looks out on the world he sees a distorted world and when people look at him through the window they see a distorted person. But it's the glass, not the person, and when the house of life is left, the person walks out as himself. That is to say, the essential personality is untouched, whether the illness was caused physically or through distorted emotional conflicts.

Yes, I can see that. But, you have said that a lot of mental illness is due to a physical cause. That's not quite what you meant, is it?

Well, as I read about it and talk with the people I work with in our clinic, there appear to be two kinds of schizophrenia or "split personality." There is the schizophrenia which is physically caused and can be physically cured, which is due to brain structures and the situation in the physical brain. This is sometimes cured by drugs, sometimes by E.C.T., which is an electric shock treatment. To go back to our illustration, the glass in the windows is made clear and the patient sees a normal world, and the world sees a normal patient.

44

Yes, I see. You mean it's caused simply through physical ill-health.

Yes. Therefore this has no relevance in the life after death. There seems to be another kind of schizophrenia which is caused through emotional conflicts which are aggravated in a patient who is perhaps mentally unstable anyway, and this I am quite sure is relieved when the emotions don't have to be repressed in a body. They are free too, just as the soul is free, though they may need sorting out. For instance, the fact of dying will not automatically remove an emotion like guilt or hate. John Smith will still be John Smith, not Saint John Smith!

Would you say that we shall be able to recognize people we have known only by repute, people of earlier generations, etc.?

Well, of course, I don't know. The only evidence in the New Testament that I can recall is that Jesus is said to have had communion with Moses and Elijah on the mount of transfiguration (Matthew 17:1-8). So He seemed to be able to come into contact with people of earlier generations. I would imagine that it is possible. But I think that there must be some link other than mere curiosity to see what the great are like and so on. Wouldn't you think that there must be some linking of souls, in the same way as we speak of "kindred spirits"? I would have thought there must be. It's difficult to understand exactly what happens, but if two persons are sufficiently attracted to each other, the length of time that one person has been in the next world should not necessarily deter them from meeting.

Will time, as we now understand it, have any part in the afterlife?

I find that a very difficult question, because for the life of me I cannot imagine a timeless existence any more than I can imagine a spaceless existence. It may well be that time in the life after death has not the same relationship as it has now to us. That is to say, we may have equal access to the past, present, and even the future. But inasmuch as I am now alive on this earth and at some point in time will pass through into another phase of existence, there must be a difference, surely, to those on the other side between the "now" to me and to them. I mean there must be some point at which I enter their world, and it must be a point in time, as I now understand time, surely.

Yes, but not time as we now understand it, because time as we now understand it is man-created.

Man gave the day its twenty-four hours because of the rising and the setting of the sun, and then grouped the days into weeks and the weeks into months and the months to form a year. I don't think time in that way will apply in the next life as far as I can imagine it.

You mean that in the next life you will not say, "I will meet you next Thursday afternoon"? And yet I can't myself imagine any phase of existence where time has no meaning at all. For example there must come a time (to use the word) when God's plan for man is completed.

Yes, don't you think space is similar? Space must be something very different in the next world from what we know it to be here. One imagines and speculates that the spirit does not occupy space, so that an etheric body is independent of space as we know it.

Dr. Weatherhead, what part, if any, does memory of events in this life play in the life after death?

Well, you remember the parable of Dives and Lazarus and how Abraham says to Dives, "Son, remember that you in your lifetime received your good things and Lazarus in like manner evil things" and now the situation is reversed, or words to that effect (Luke 16:25). Apparently, if we are not claiming too much from the language used, memory does go on, and one would imagine that part of one's purgatory is to remember with regret the things that one has done that are wrong. I would also have thought that part of one's purgatory was to suffer with any person one had wronged until that person forgave one and thus purged the evil which had been wrought. I am rather afraid that memory *will* go on and it will be very painful to remember some things, just as it will be heaven to remember some other things, like the experi-

47

ence of loving, serving, and the enjoyment one had in beauty. Do you remember the poem (I think I can recite it to you) that was written originally by Bishop Stubbs?

> I sat alone with my Conscience
>   In a place where time had ceased.
> We discoursed of my former living
>   In a land where the years increased,
> And I felt I should have to answer
>   The questions it put to me,
> And to face those questions and answers
>   In that dim eternity.
> And the ghosts of forgotten actions
>   Came floating before my sight,
> And the sins that I thought were dead sins
>   Were alive with a terrible might.
> And I know of the future Judgment,
>   How dreadful so e'er it be,
> That to sit alone with my conscience
>   Would be judgment enough for me!

That says rather a lot, doesn't it?

Yes. It emphasizes that the memory of sin committed in this world may torture you in the next. But surely if one has repented of one's sins here and accepted forgiveness, these are obliterated and cease to disturb one?

Yes, I think this is a very important point and I am so glad you raised it. Forgiveness restores relationship, and there is plenty of evidence of that in the Bible.

"I will forgive their iniquity and their sin will I remember no more" (Jeremiah 31:34). "As far as the east is from the west, so far hath He removed our transgressions from us" (Psalm 103:12).

At the same time, as I try to meditate on the point I feel that in the next phase of being, if clearer light on sin is granted to me, I shall still be bitterly ashamed that I ever hurt my loving Father by doing the things that I did. And although penalty is obliterated—the penalty of sin being separation from God—although I am one with Him, surely I shall still deeply regret that I ever did what I did and bear scars that can't be completely eradicated? Forgiveness does not obliterate consequences, though it alters them from resented pain to accepted discipline.

Do you know what I mean? The prodigal comes home again, and the relationship is restored. At once he is a son; he is back at home. But surely he still bears the scars of his adventures, perhaps in his body but certainly in his mind and his spirit, and thinks, "However did I come to hurt my father like that? " Wouldn't that become the source of new energy to serve with greater devotion? God can make of *forgiven* sin a qualification and asset with which one can help others similarly tempted.

Yes. Do you think that is why without the father having to say a word—no condemnation, no inquiry—the prodigal just knew that he was forgiven and accepted?

Yes, this is so. Judgment to me is never the judgment

imposed by a judge on a throne who tells a trembling sinner that he is hell-bound.

Judgment to me, in the realm of religion, means judgment we pass on ourselves in the light of Christ's love and God's long-suffering in giving mercy.

In the life after death has sin any place at all?

Here again one is speculating. I can't understand how the accident of death, as it often is, can make one incapable of sinning. If one has free will and choice, surely there must be a measure of temptation, the overcoming of which is the basis of one's growth. I can understand that as one grows spiritually and understands more of what God's nature is, and what His love involves, one is less and less tempted. I can't understand how a person until he really achieves perfection and unity with God can be, as it were, automatically made sinless by the accident of dying. And although having lost one's body one isn't tempted to certain types of sin, and since one is not in possession of any material thing there is no temptation to steal, I would have thought that there could still have been a temptation to pride or jealousy or envy or resentment, or even hate.

4. HOW CAN WE PREPARE OURSELVES?

*Can you tell us how we can best prepare ourselves for
the next life? We seem to be more occupied in making
ourselves comfortable in this one. This seems to be our
main concern—getting all the pleasures we can out
of this life, mainly physical pleasures. How then can
we best prepare ourselves for the next?*

This is where Christ's coming into our lowly flesh
has tremendous importance. The final goal of life after
death is to be one with God, to be fitted to share His
amazing, glorious life. Then the sooner we give up
concentrating on values such as you have hinted at,
in being comfortable, sqeezing the last drop of pleasure
out of life for ourselves, attaining high rank and important positions, the sooner we see that it is more
important to develop character, develop capacity for
God, the better it will be for us.

We are so often the victims of a faulty sense of
values. Dr. Temple once said it as though somebody
got into a shop in the night and altered the price labels
of the things in the shop, so that valuable things were
marked low, and useless things were marked high. Now
that is exactly what has happened in this life. Things
like obligation, service to others, a sense of duty, unself-
ish sacrifice, humility—these things are marked low.
But having a good time, gaining your ends, socially, sex-
ually, materially, academically—these are marked high.
This is one of the things that is wrong with the world.
It's living as though there were nothing else after death
and this is wrong or—to say the least—mistaken. Belief in survival helps us to get our sense of values right.

51

Man has been on earth a very long time and doesn't seem to be making very much progress in soul growth.

No. And yet think of the days when a man was hung for stealing 1s. 6d.; think of the days when boys of thirteen were working in the mines for twelve, thirteen, and fourteen hours a day; think how a man was sacked ruthlessly, and left without any unemployment benefit or State aid because he displeased a tyrannical boss. We have made progress in things like these. Think of the days of slavery when slaves were the property of the owners; and men could rape the girl slaves and beat a slave to death. From that kind of ruthless cruelty and barbarity there has been tremendous progress in the modern period.

But not on the same scale as progress in physical and scientific spheres.

No, I'm afraid not.

But if we are now already spirits, or souls, whatever the term is, what do we do that hinders our soul's growth?

Surely what would hinder our soul's growth would be a concentration on things that have no significance after death. I mean if I put all my energies into getting rich, if I put all my energies into academic accomplishments, if I put them all into attaining social status, into being a little bit better than the Joneses, this is no kind of preparation for the next world.

But if, on the other hand, I put my emphasis into

trying to serve other people, comforting the distressed, helping the troubled, working for the brotherhood of all mankind and so on—serving my fellows—that is giving me better qualifications for the next world.

Could you enlarge on what happens to our souls if we don't feed them?

Surely the answer is that we shall enter the other life, where spiritual values are more clearly seen to be important, like a teacher, shall we say, who wants to teach but fails his degrees. We shall be in an inferior condition to function in the next world, but we may still be allowed to go on making progress and forsake the false ideals of our earlier life. Or we may indeed— and this is only an opinion (but it is shared by about five million other people, all the Hindus and Buddhists)—be allowed to come back and take the exams again in another incarnation. I find nothing in this idea to conflict with the Christian faith and I find a lot in it that makes sense of some of the anomalies and apparent injustices of this life.

Yes, but I don't want at this stage to go into reincarnation. I am rather more concerned in the encouragement of soul growth and what happens if we neglect the soul. You have used analogies in the past of what would happen to our physical bodies if we were to neglect any part of them. For example, if we were blindfolded for long periods our eyes could become useless. Is this applicable as well to our souls?

53

Yes, I think so. Just as eyes need light, just as the lungs need air, just as the ears need sound, just as the mind needs truth, so the spirit or the soul needs communion with God. Because the eyes need light, because light is the only environment in which they can function, if light is cut off they atrophy, and the same is true in the other cases I have hinted at. If you cut yourself off from God and things spiritual altogether, your soul diminishes in its power to live, so that if you are thrust suddenly by death into a spiritual world you are like a half-blind man confronted with a sunset. Or I would say you are like a tone-deaf man who finds he is in a marvelous concert which other people who have developed their musical faculties and their hearing can appreciate, but it is boring and meaningless to him.

Can you think of any other illustrations of things which might hinder soul growth? For example, if I give way to certain temptations, whether just bad temper or sexual desire, and can say to myself, "Well, I think I won't count this time; it doesn't matter this time," does this have any effect?

Surely it does. Somebody once said, "God will forgive you, but your nervous system won't." That is to say, if you plunge into, say sex-deviations and extravagances, increasing physical desire, and then you pass over into a world where the physical does not exist, you have increased something which cannot function there, to the detriment of your spirit. But if you strengthen the spirit by prayer, by meditation, and by loving others, you increase your capacity to enjoy life. Does that seem clear?

Yes, but I would like some more examples.

Let me put it this way. Two men go to a concert; one is a musician to his finger tips; he has studied music, he loves music, great music played by great artists is heaven to him. He sits next to a man who is tone deaf, to whom music means nothing, and who sits there just wishing for the interval when he can have a drink, something that he *can* enjoy. Now, they are sitting next to each other, but between them there is a great gulf fixed. Jesus talked about a great gulf being fixed (Luke 16:26). It may not be fixed forever, but it is fixed for the time being, inasmuch as the musician cannot inject his friend with the love of music. His friend, supposing the concert went on forever, could begin to be taught how to enjoy music. Now this, to me, is the difference between Heaven and Hell. Surely, Heaven to the spiritual man is like a good concert to the musical man; he feels "This is where I belong, this is marvelous, this is life to me." Hell, surely, is to be in a situation where one is bored and there is nothing left to enjoy, and where one suffers remorse at one's own shortsightedness.

I would like to come back to what you have just been saying, because I am sure there is great value in the idea that you have given about the two friends going to a concert, one being able to appreciate the music and one not being able to. But while we are considering factors which might harm soul growth, can you think of any other illustrations?

There is one which comes to my mind, which I have quoted before, concerning putting off till tomorrow or some later date the determination to put right in ourselves what we know to be wrong. I can remember staying with a man in the Lake District, when I was the fellow-guest with another minister. He and I were talking about poetry. Now this host of ours was a very charming, generous, and lovable man, but his life was mainly given up to making his business a success. Overhearing us he said, "You know, when I retire I am going to take up poetry."

Now, you cannot do that. You cannot deny a culture like poetry, music, or art until you are about seventy and say, "Go to, I will now enjoy poetry." And it is highly dangerous to say, "Well, I am going to have a right good time here; I am going to give way to all my instincts; I am going to make money and enjoy myself thoroughly on the physical plane; and when I see death looming up, I will jolly well switch over to spiritual things." Of course it is better to switch over than not to do so, but we must not expect to catch up at once with the man who has been a life-long saint.

So it is essential as early as possible to direct our thoughts to spiritual things and to be concerned by spiritual problems. Now, how best can we do this?

You know as well as I do all the devotional aids, like prayer, meditation, the Bible, and other good literature, corporate worship, and Christian fellowship. I would very much like also to get in a word here that there are a lot of things in life that are religious that are not *labeled* religious. I object to the idea that saying prayers, going to church, reading the Bible, are necessarily more spiritually enriching than, say, a great concert, great poetry, or the love of nature. God fulfills Himself in many ways. Anything that makes the spirit of man respond to beauty or truth or love or goodness, is enriching to his soul, and through these things he can increase his spiritual stature.

I said I would revert to the analogy of the two friends going to a concert, one being able to appreciate good music and the other not. I think there may be some danger in laboring appreciation of the arts because, am I not right in thinking that there are other things of the spirit—a relationship with Christ for example, or a relationship with a good man—which can do a bad man a lot of good? Have you anything to say on that?

Yes. Clearly the whole heart of Christianity is a relationship with the living Christ. The very word "religion" means "a link," the ligament, the thing that binds you to something else, and it is this relationship which is nourished by prayer and religious meditation and so on.

Would you not say that in this is the number one essential for spiritual growth?

Yes, I was using the concert only as an illustration. The man who loves Christ starts in the next world with an enormous advantage over the man to whom Christ is a meaningless word. People noticed in the disciples a transformation, and they attributed it to the fact that they had been with Christ (Acts 4:13). This we should all endeavor to do during our daily lives. The more time we can spend in a conscious relationship with Christ the better we become.

Can you give us some more illustrations of what would help us to grow spiritually, since this is the only thing that really matters in life?

Yes, but there is a danger in separating secular and sacred and saying, "I grow more, spiritually, by meditation and thinking about Christ than in doing my daily work." There is a catch here. It may be the calling, the vocation, of some people to be monks or to be nuns, but Jesus never made this kind of distinction between sacred and secular. I don't think a thing is made secular by what it is but by the way you do it. A person who runs a home so that all the wheels run smoothly and you do not hear them grinding; a person who spends life ministering to people within that home; a person who, like yourself, is serving other people's needs; this is as sacred, it seems to me, in the eyes of Christ, as giving people Holy Communion or preaching sermons.

I am not quite sure that that is what I meant. I am recalling what Edward Wilson once wrote to the ef-

fect that if we were to give as much time to our spiritual well-being as we give to our physical well-being mankind would make terrific strides forward. He gives the illustration that we get up in the morning and bathe and feed and clothe ourselves, and look after the comforts of physical well-being, but a vast majority of us have no concern at all for spiritual well-being.

Yes, indeed. I am sure we ought to spend more time in spiritual culture. But you can see my own argument if you take it to an extreme. Here is a man who sits in his study, let us say, and declares, "I will spend today in spiritual culture for my own soul," and by so doing rejects an invitation to go and help someone who is bereaved, or says "No" to a person who says, "I am ill; will you come and see me."

I couldn't agree with you more. It seems to me we are out of balance. We are giving far too much time to our physical well-being and far too little to our spiritual, and our spiritual well-being must include service to others.

We are often asked if it is morbid for young people to think about death. My answer would be, "Of course not." Natural death is as normal as birth. Both are within God's Plan. I think it is essential for their soul growth and personality that young people should think about death. Death is a mystery; life is a mystery, life on earth is full of mystery. Plant life, animal life, bird life, fish life, every wave of the ocean, every star that shines—each has its own hidden mystery. Life

59

*hereafter is also a mystery, God's mystery, full of
blessings. Why then should young people be turned
away from the greatest and best of all mysteries? Why
should young people not seriously contemplate the
incomparably great and unseen life which lies before
them and into which they must inevitably embark
someday? There is nothing morbid in that. It would
only be morbid and unwholesome if they thought that
death was the end, but it is not. Do you agree with me?*

Well, in part. I think it would be morbid if young
people full of life and bursting with energy and happiness; loving and being loved, for instance, *continually*
allowed their minds to dwell on death. I think that
would be morbid. I can only go back to my own
experience. I am sure that as a teen-ager and a young
man I didn't let my mind dwell on death. I think
however that from time to time it is a good thing
if people are challenged with the fact that one must
die sometime.

A very dear friend of mine was in an office which
was bombed and everybody was killed except herself.
She was covered with other people's blood and had
a very terrible experience. She said to me, "On that
day I decided that I would always try to live each day
as if it were my last." Now that was not morbid. I
think the whole idea that death was very near and did
not touch her has influenced her for good. From time
to time it's a very good thing if all of us come to
terms with the idea of death, rob it of its terrors,
think our way through the problem and so on. As

you say, it is as natural as birth. But to be quite honest and down to earth I would think that a teen-ager, healthy and full of beans, would be morbid if he let his mind continually dwell on death. Don't you agree?

It depends. You spoke about the time when you were young. I think the thought of death was handled differently and I think wrongly during that period. If somebody died everybody was so solemn. The black mourning clothes, the pulling down of the blinds— they made it a morbid thing. It should be a joyous thing, I think, and unless we do realize that there is something after this life, we are never going to build up our personalities, our characters, our souls. This is what I have been pushing so strongly all the way through our conversation, that we must be living now to prepare ourselves for the life after this.

Yes, but could you not by that teaching induce too great an introspective preoccupation with your own soul and how it was getting on? A man at university, for example, knows that he is preparing for his professional life, but he does not really spend much time thinking what it will be like when he is qualified. He's playing rugger and going to dances and enjoying life to the full, as well as attending classes.

Yes, and rightly so. Of course one has to keep all things in balance, but it's my contention that we don't give nearly enough time to thinking about the life that follows this one.

5. WHAT IF WE ARE NOT CHRISTIANS?

Some things which Jesus said about life after death can be understood by most people. But what about phrases like "I am the bread of life and if any man eat of this bread he shall live for ever"? (John 6:51.) Suppose a man were not a Christian, but a Jew or a Hindu, and did not understand. What happens to such people? They need a life after death, too, don't they?

Yes, of course. I think the only answer I can give is, I don't know what happens to them. I am sure that life after death contains further choices, further visions, of what is ultimately desirable, so that the Jew and what we used to call the heathen—Mohammedan, Buddhist, Hindu—finds everything that was true in his religion justified. But I also believe that he finds Christ to be someone who can reveal even more to him, so that he doesn't have to deny anything that was true in his Jewish religion, Hindu religion or Mohammedan religion, and yet finds Christ offering him further insight and understanding of what communion with God means. It is like a man climbing the foothills of the Himalayas and then finding the shining heights still beyond him. With the vision will come a burning desire to climb still higher. Christ is the summit of the Hindu road as He is of the Christian way. I do not believe that because a man has not been a Christian he perishes at death, if that is what you mean. I won't believe that for a moment.

Yet this seems to be what the words of Christ imply, but they are probably minunderstood. "I am the bread of life and if any man eat of this bread he shall live forever" seems rather to rule out the others. Do people of other faiths believe in life after death?

Indeed they do.

Of all other faiths?

As far as I know, they do. The Mohammedan believes, doesn't he, that he will be welcomed by dusky maidens and have a wonderful life with them; the Hindu believes that he will come back and be incarnated in other and presumably higher forms of life. I do not know any religion that asserts that man is finished by the accident of dying. This would seem to me absolutely irrational.

In your opinion, Dr. Weatherhead, will all be won for God in the end?

Well, there are people in various churches who would deny what I believe. They think that death does determine what happens to you and that the righteous go into what they call everlasting life, and that the wicked go into hell, I suppose. Now I can't understand this, and I am not just speculating without any basis. Paul says, God "willeth that all should be saved and come to the knowledge of the truth" (I Timothy 2:4). A greater authority still, Jesus, when He gives us the

63

parables of the Lost Sheep and the Lost Coin and the Lost Son (Luke 15), uses in two of those stories the words "until he find it." The shepherd goes over the mountain and looks for the sheep "until he find it"; the woman looks for the coin "until she find it"; the ever-loving father is unhappy about the prodigal until he comes home. "As in Adam all die," says Paul, "so in Christ shall *all* be made alive" (I Corinthians 15:22).

Now I don't see how God who is Love can be satisfied if there is one soul in an endless hell, if there is one soul lost. That is a defeat of eternal purpose and that I don't believe is possible. I don't know how many phases of life on the other side of death are involved or how long it will take or what will happen. But I can't believe that even any *human* person capable of love can be in perfect bliss if there is one soul in endless unhappiness and grief and pain. How much less can God be content? So I don't think there will be heaven—not the highest heaven—for anybody, least of all for God, unless we are all in it.

Can a Christian wife hope to meet and recognize her husband who has died having made no profession of faith at all, and perhaps having denied having any faith?

I think the answer must be that if she loves her husband and her husband loves her they will be reunited and have fellowship together. One must not suppose that the life after death is, so to speak, all within the field of religion, as we understand it, any more than this life is.

You see, people recognize that this life is a tremendously complex system of communication with other people who by and large have no reference to religion at all. I do not see why we should regard life after death only in a religious context. I think religion is equally and even more important, but I think some people imagine that the next world will be like attendance at one very long service in a church. I should hate that and so would you.

It's quite indisputable that we are all going to die, and to my way of thinking we are all going to live again in the next world, whether we are members of any church or any faith or no faith.

I think so, too.

What about people who never attain to communion with God at all?

If the soul was cut off entirely from any contact with God, the logic of the situation would be that the soul would die. Science, at any rate, knows nothing of an organism which is permanently cut off from its environment and yet goes on living.

But I would have thought that even those people who have repudiated religion as we understand and have experienced it are nevertheless able to come into

65

touch with God. Every time they admire a sunset they are in communion with God; every time they serve a neighbor they are in communion with God; every time they respond to the love of a child they are in communion with God.

I think that we have got to be very careful not to limit communion with God to the framework provided by religion. Bernard Shaw said, "There is as much healing power in a Beethoven Sonata or a painting by Constable as there is in some excerpts from the Bible." I believe this is true, and I am sure that many a devoted Christian thinks that if he reads a psalm through at night, this is a religious activity, but that if he listens receptively to beautiful music, that is not a religious thing to do. Surely this distinction is false. I think we agree that any sensitive contact with beauty, truth, love, or goodness is an experience of God.

6. AT THE VERY END

Dr. Weatherhead, as I understand some religious teachers, they speak about a final judgment. Could you comment and explain that to some degree?

I don't think that there is such a thing as a final judgment. If a spirit remains free, this means that he's always free to choose, and to say that any choice must be his final choice seems to me a contradiction of that freedom. My own view is that God wills that every living soul shall at last be brought by free choice into harmony with His will. I understand that it may be aeons of time, as we think of time, before everyone is brought in. But the Bible seems to be very strong on this point that all shall be saved and come to a knowledge of the truth. So I believe that finally, without any coercion or any unfair use of force, the soul will come to see that its highest welfare is in saying "Yes" to God. And that finally this will happen and all created beings will be brought into harmony with God, in an ultimate heaven the nature of which we simply haven't the power to imagine.

Is it right to assume that at death man wishes to pursue his highest ideals? And if not, is this the difference between Heaven and Hell?

Yes, I think it is. On the one hand a good man with ideals which he wishes to realize finds himself in a sphere in which he can more and more ably express those ideals. But a man who at death has no great desire to express his highest nature may find himself in the very strange and painful situation in which the only things he can do are those he has no desire to do. It seems to me this is the kind of difference between Heaven and Hell.

But this is not necessarily his final state?

I do not see why it should be. The man who is thoroughly bored with music, for example, can begin to learn music. So surely death doesn't determine our *final* destiny? Surely a man in another world—let's take this illustration of music—where he finds music is the great reality and the source of joy begins (*a*) to wish that he had paid more attention to it earlier and (*b*) begins to listen to it and study it so that he can appreciate it.

As for judgment, I never think of this as a great white throne where God says to one man, "You are for everlasting life" and to another man, "You are to be in an endless Hell." Judgment is passed upon us by the nature of the sphere in which we find ourselves. Let's pursue further the analogy of the concert which we used before. The two men who go to the concert are judged by the music. Nobody comes on to the stage and says, "You're no good because you can't appreciate it, and *you* are marvelous because you can." The music itself judges the person by whether he is at home with it or bored by it.

This is what Jesus meant when he said He did not

come to judge the world but to save the world (John 12:47). Then according to the Fourth Gospel He added, "The word that I spake, the same shall judge him in the last day" (v. 48). To me every day, in a sense, is a judgment day. When beauty or truth or goodness or love confront you and you love them and respond to them and accept them and would like to develop them, then you are judged as a lover of these things. If they bore you or you think they are valueless, then they condemn you.

Dr. Weatherhead, when you were talking about a final judgment, you said that a soul is free and has the power of choice. But does there ever come a time when finally there is no choice for him?

I can't conceive that there can ever be a time when a spirit with free will is doomed and has no further chance of finding God. For one thing it would be a divine failure. If one single soul loved of God, as well as loved by other people, passed into nothingness, this would be a divine defeat.

I think that there can never come a time when a soul cannot turn to God and begin to live more fully. I suppose theoretically we have to say that the soul could go on saying "No" to God. But I cannot bring myself to believe that that can ever be final because, as I say, that is a defeat for God and it is the loss of a precious soul, and it denies one of the essential qualities in the soul which must surely be free will. Although you can say, theoretically, that he could always choose

69

darkness, darkness, darkness, darkness and never choose light, surely as he goes through all the training in God's further schools for the soul after this life, he will be brought to the point where he longs for the light, and will respond to God. Maybe he had never before seen light as beautiful and desirable.

Yes, and will gradually come out of the pitch darkness into gray and then another shade of darkness until he must eventually progress forward. Not necessarily quickly, but God has plenty of time.

You see, we talk about a defeat of God. But surely there cannot be Heaven for anybody if *one soul* is debarred from entering it? Even if it is his own fault. If a person is run over in the street and it is entirely his own fault, you don't refuse to take him to hospital and get him better. In the infinitely more crucial situation of a soul's eternal welfare the same principle must surely apply. However much the fault is ours, and in greater or less measure it always is, the love of God will never cease to try to win us.

So this means that no choice a soul makes will in fact prove final because God Himself will not accept it as final?

No, because God Himself will not accept it as final.

7. REINCARNATION?

Dr. Weatherhead, can Christians believe in reincarnation?

Well, now, this is a question which is rather amusingly phrased. It reminds me of a question that Dr. Maltby was asked years ago, "Can Christians dance?" and he said, "Well, some can and some can't," and he added, "I have often been the victim of those who can't! Now to be serious, can Christians believe in reincarnation? I think they can. That is to say, I don't see anything in this theory which contradicts the Christian position. In our Lord's time it was part of the accepted beliefs of everybody. Indeed, it was accepted by the Christian Church until 553 when the Council of Constantinople rejected it by a very narrow majority. And, after all, five hundred million Buddhists and Hindus accept the idea of reincarnation. To brush away an idea tenaciously held by such an enormous number of our fellows, including some very great saints and scholars, seems to me a thing one should hesitate to do.

It attracts me because it seems to me to make sense of some situations which otherwise seem terribly unjust and beyond understanding. And I would say that it forms a background to the Gospels. You may remember that the Fourth Gospel records the disciples coming to Jesus with the man born blind—I underline *born* blind—and they say, "Who did sin, this man, or his parents, that he was born blind?" (John 9:2). Jesus says "Neither," and he proceeds to a very interesting answer which is not relevant to the particular question we are considering. But if a man is *born* blind and the possible cause of his blindness is sin, as the disciples obviously believed possible, it must have been sin in an earlier life. That makes sense, doesn't it?

It does, yes.

Furthermore, on another occasion the disciples come to Jesus and Jesus says to them, "Who do men say that I am?" and they answer, "Some say John the Baptist; some Elijah: and others Jeremiah or one of the prophets" (Matthew 16:13, 14). Well now, I know that it is not very convincing to regard silence as conclusive, but it is very remarkable that He doesn't say, "Don't talk nonsense." He seems to accept that it is possible that He Himself could have been a reincarnation of one of these men.

I could give you case after case of the most amazing things that have happened for which I can't find any other explanation than that of reincarnation. For instance, Sir William Hamilton at thirteen could speak thirteen languages. Though just a boy, he wrote a letter to the Persian ambassador. The diplomat read it and then said, "Look, this is not modern Persian; this is ancient script of the Persian language which passed out of use years ago." Now how on earth did this boy know ancient Persian?

Then you have the boy who was tremendously excited in the British Museum by the sarcophagi, the stone coffins, and said that in an earlier life he himself had been an inspector of these coffins. He went on to say that if one he indicated were turned over, they would find his own mark of the fish underneath it. They persuaded the attendant to turn it over, and there were the marks of the fish.

Or you have the boy who was going over some ruins when he was on holiday with his mother and suddenly seemed very emotionally disturbed at being shown some caves in which prisoners had been walled up. He said there was another prisoner further along this cliff side. But the guide said, "No, no, it isn't so, these are all there are." But excavation showed that the boy was right, and they broke open this old cave which had been walled up, and they found the skeleton behind it.

There are so many other cases of that kind. A child was found singing a French cradle-song before she was capable of learning, or had had any opportunity of hearing the French language. Again and again you come across this kind of knowledge. Then there are cases of the genius, and the prodigy whose ability seems to me most adequately accounted for by the fact that he has lived before.

The child prodigy you mean? The great musician and the great mathematician as a child, for example?

Yes. I have been in correspondence lately with the mother of a little girl who, at eight years of age, faultlessly conducted a Beethoven Symphony with the London Symphony Orchestra. *The Times* commented that "our only concern is that such a strain should be placed on a child so young." Now, why, why should she be able to do this? Plato said that the genius is the man for whom knowledge and ability flow back easily because they have been there before. I could give you authority for whom this is an established part of the truth; and I don't think it does any despite to the Christian religion, and I think it lights up some phases of it which otherwise are so very dark.

Still on this question of reincarnation, earlier you explained that if we did not die a physical death this planet of ours would become hopelessly overpopulated, and we therefore pass into the realm of the spirit. But there are thousands of millions of people who die. How can they possibly all live in the spirit world? Would reincarnation in a sense depopulate the spirit world?

I think there is a catch in this because we are assuming that spirit occupies space. Even so people also find it very hard to think that God can care about all the people who have died and exist in the spirit world. I am helped here by this fact. There are more cells in your brain at this moment than there are people in this world, and yet all those cells in your brain have a function and importance, and if anything happened to a few of them you would soon know about it. Now may it not be true that, as the Bible says, "In Him we live"? (Acts 17:28.) May it be that our relationship to God is not a relationship of, for example, ants on an ant-heap, with a superior being looking down upon them and trying to keep interested in their doings? May it not be that the illustration of the brain is closer to the truth, that is to say that we are to God as the cells of our brain are to us; that we are in a very real sense part of Him and that He is expressing His life through us and that each one of us therefore is precious to Him for His sake as well as for ours?

I think this is of value. I think also that what you have just said is true, that spirits pass into the next world and they may very well return into a physical existence. But not because there isn't room for them. After all even if they *were* physical, the universe now is seen to be such an incredibly enormous thing that one imagines there is plenty of room on other planets. But I rather feel we are saying a more important thing when we say that the spirit as such does not take up any more space than your love for your wife takes up space. That's a thing of the spirit. It seems to me possible, however, that some people may *have* to come back, some people may *want* to come back, some people may *choose* to come back to serve the world.

I have a speculation that Jesus may have been a spirit very highly developed, perhaps through innumerable reincarnations who, as the hymn says, from His throne on high, seeing our miserable plight, offered to come back and take on our flesh in order to help us and bring us to God.

Quintin Hogg wrote recently that it is the young nurse ministering to the sick in hospital; the teacher seeking to give conscious life and happiness to the mentally handicapped child; the probation officer struggling to save the young delinquent from a life of crime; the surgeon battling at the operating theater for the life of a patient; the nun or Salvation Army lass in the Leper Colony—it is such people as these who in reality give inspiration and guidance and insight into the nature of God, not those who resort to the Hindu form of meditation deliberately cultivated to turn the individual in on himself and to disregard the suffering of others. I wholeheartedly agree with him, don't you?

Yes, I certainly do, and I am sure Christianity at its best is superior to Hinduism in the way you indicated. At the same time I think the Hindu religion has an enormous amount to teach us. I don't feel that one can cast aside the beliefs of a large part of the human race as though that religion had nothing to offer, and I think it has a lot to say to us in the matter of reincarnation. I think that the idea of reincarnation is a sound one. I mentioned just now that it was part of the teaching of the Christian Church for some centuries. It was an accepted idea, and I think it throws light on a great many problems that Christianity as popularly understood doesn't deal with.

Such as what?

Well, I think that one of the basic ideas of the Christian religion is that God is just. Finally, no one will

76

be able to turn on God with the accusation, "I have suffered from injustice all my life. Why should so-and-so be born into a wealthy family and have all the privileges of a happy life with everything needed, supplied, and why should I have this and that disadvantage?" Now, if we take this life by itself, it's very hard to exonerate God from the charge of injustice. But if life was lived before this one and goes on after this one, then one can say to people suffering from a sense of injustice, "When you can look at the whole of your being, you will grant that life was after all just." For what appeared to be the injustice at one phase was the result of an earlier phase. What looks like fate or luck or accident, may be a just purposefulness not yet understood. Reincarnation really does make sense of life and I feel there is no other way of exonerating God from the charge of injustice and cruelty.

Think, for example, of all those children cursed in the Aberfan disaster when a coal-tip overwhelmed their school. We can find comfort in the thought that they will live again and that life is indestructible. The horizon is so extended that the perspective is altered, just as the tragedies of our childhood seem different now that we have grown up.

Because thousands swept away in a disaster will live in another favored life, this doesn't necessarily strengthen the argument for reincarnation, because reincarnation surely means that one can be born back on to this planet, doesn't it?

It is generally thought of as life lived again on this planet, but I don't think that is essentially so. If the word reincarnation means "in the flesh" it isn't perhaps the best word, because other people on other planets may express themselves in other forms than flesh. But the idea for me is full of meaning because the only way we can bear the thought of these natural disasters like earthquakes and tidal waves, storms and so on is that these people somewhere and at some time will live again, and that sudden death in an age-long perspective will only be like moving from one residence to another.

And this is how the belief in reincarnation lights up the Christian religion?

Yes. If you say that this life is only one form in God's school, and you will pass into another form and find that all you have suffered here has become an asset for another alife—not necessarily a life in the spirit but another life in the flesh or in some other manifestation—this is where the idea of reincarnation comes in.

Are there any examples that you could give to enlarge on this?

Well, surely there must be a great many tests you can only pass while life is in the flesh. So if you fail those tests it seems to be irrelevant to pass into a life that is purely spiritual. You have got to take those tests again in the flesh.

78

Yes, such as. . . ?

The person who has given vent to his sexual appetites and crushed other people's lives in so doing; the person who has amassed material wealth by means of being unfair to others and trampling on them—these are tests that he has failed to pass and which can be passed only in a material set-up.

That is why he has to take on again a material body of some kind?

Yes. But having said that, I am bound to confess I am not convinced that there is, for example, *no* sex in the next life which could be experienced without coming back here. But I am not sure about this, and I don't suppose anybody can be.

Except that there is something akin to love and affection in the next world. But it is very hard to believe that sex, which is largely a physical desire, like that of the hungry to eat food, can be felt by a person who is not in a body.

Yes. There must obviously be sex since there must be male and female; but not physical sex as we express it here. That is the probable answer.

And one would rather hope that it is sublimated into a kind of spiritual love.

79

Yes, as Jesus implied when He said that in the next life there will be no marriage but we shall be (as we noticed earlier) "like angels in heaven."

I want to end on this positive note. We need never think of death as gloomy and forbidding. It may seem natural to do so. But if we had been able to anticipate this present life in the period before birth, we should have felt the same foreboding. Yet in fact there was nothing to fear. Love and care were waiting for us. We can rest assured that God who provided for us when we began this life will do no less as we pass from it. The place prepared for us, of which Jesus spoke, will surely include happy reunions and fresh and thrilling adventures.

One day it will be our turn to move on to a new plane of life. Away with our fears! Think of it as like leaving for a holiday in a country we have never visited before. Let us only make sure we have time to pack the things we shall *need*, and get ready.

So be my passing!
My task accomplished and the long day done,
My wages taken, and in my heart
Some late lark singing,
Let me be gathered to the quiet west,
The sundown splendid and serene,
Death.

W. E. Henley